SUPER STRIKERS

Written by Mark Hillsdon

The publisher would like to thank the following for their kind permission to reproduce their photographs:

a=above; b=below; c=centre; l=left; r=right; t=top.

ACTION-PLUS: Glyn Kirk *Shearer* sidebar, 5bc, 7bc, 11tc, 12bc, 18c; Neil Tingle 8tc, 14c, 15bc, 17tc, 21bc.

ACTION-PLUS/FLASH PRESS: 26tc.

ALLSPORT: 3bc; Clive Brunskill 9tc, 22bc; David Cannon 20c; David Leah 24bc; Gary M Prior 16tc; Mark Thompson 10bc; Ben Radford 2tc, 28cr.

EMPICS: Matthew Ashton 19bc; Tony Marshall 27bc; Neal Simpson 29tr.

FRONT COVER
ACTION-PLUS: br; Neil Tingle c;
EMPICS: Valeria Witters cla.

PICTURE RESEARCHER: Catherine Costelloe.

All information correct at time of going to press.

FUNFAX™

Copyright © 1998 Henderson Publishing Ltd

FRANCE

WELCOME TO THE WORLD CUP!

France 1998 is quite simply the biggest World Cup ever! The World Cup is held every four years and this time more than 100 countries, from every corner of the globe, entered the qualifying tournament. Now 32 teams are left to compete in the finals between June 14 and July 12 1998. That's 64 matches in total, compared with just 18 at the first World Cup in Uruguay, held as long ago as 1930!

As well as being the largest tournament ever, France 1998 is only the third time that the same country has staged the finals more than once. France were also hosts in 1938; Italy and Mexico have also held the championships twice.

A player's international experience is based on the following code:

0–15 CAPS ★
16–30 CAPS ★ ★
31–45 CAPS ★ ★ ★
46–60 CAPS ★ ★ ★ ★
61+ CAPS ★ ★ ★ ★ ★

FRANCE

NAME: Youri Djorkaeff
BORN: 9.3.68, Lyon, France
HEIGHT: 5 ft 10 (1 m 78)
CLUB SIDE: Inter Milan (Italy)
EXPERIENCE: ★ ★ ★
KEY FACT: Capable of the spectacular.
AMAZING FACT: His father Jean won 48 caps for France.

NAME: Christophe Dugarry
BORN: 24.3.72, Bordeaux, France
HEIGHT: 6 ft 2 (1 m 88)
CLUB SIDE: Marseille (France)
EXPERIENCE: ★ ★
KEY FACT: Strong in the air.

WORLD CUP 1998

3 SUPER STRIKERS

BRAZIL

NAME: 'Ronaldo' Luis Nazario De Lima
BORN: 22.9.76, Rio de Janeiro, Brazil
HEIGHT: 5 ft 11 (1 m 80)
CLUB SIDE: Inter Milan (Italy)
EXPERIENCE: ★ ★
KEY FACT: The perfect footballer, combining speed, power and skill.
AMAZING FACT: Voted FIFA World Player of the Year 1997.

4 SUPER STRIKERS

BRAZIL

NAME: 'Edmundo' Alves De Souza Neto
BORN: 2.4.71, Rio de Janeiro, Brazil
HEIGHT: 5 ft 10 (1 m 78)
CLUB SIDE: Vasco da Gama (Brazil)
EXPERIENCE: ★ ★ ★
KEY FACT: Skilful, but has a very fiery temper.
AMAZING FACT: His nickname is 'The Animal'!

NAME: Paulo Nunes – Arilson De Paula Nunes
BORN: 30.1.71, Pontalina, Brazil
HEIGHT: 5 ft 9 (1 m 75)
CLUB SIDE: Benfica (Portugal)
EXPERIENCE: ★
KEY FACT: An excellent crosser of the ball.

NAME: Romario De Souza Faria
BORN: 29.1.66, Rio de Janeiro, Brazil
HEIGHT: 5 ft 6 (1 m 68)
CLUB SIDE: Valencia (Spain)
EXPERIENCE: ★ ★ ★
KEY FACT: A predator in the penalty box.
AMAZING FACT: FIFA voted him the World's Best Player in 1994.

5 SUPER STRIKERS

ENGLAND

NAME: Alan Shearer
BORN: 13.8.70, Newcastle, England
HEIGHT: 5 ft 11 (1 m 80)
CLUB SIDE: Newcastle United (England)
EXPERIENCE: ★ ★
KEY FACT: Lethal from inside or outside the penalty area.
AMAZING FACT: Newcastle paid Blackburn £15m for Shearer, a British record.

ENGLAND

NAME: Robbie Fowler
BORN: 9.4.75, Liverpool, England
HEIGHT: 5 ft 11 (1 m 80)
CLUB SIDE: Liverpool (England)
EXPERIENCE: ★
KEY FACT: Great work rate and great finisher.
AMAZING FACT: Scored a hat trick in 4 minutes 33 seconds against Arsenal in December 1994.

NAME: Teddy Sheringham
BORN: 2.4.66, Higham Park, England
HEIGHT: 6 ft (1 m 83)
CLUB SIDE: Manchester United (England)
EXPERIENCE: ★ ★
KEY FACT: Excellent in the air.

NAME: Ian Wright
BORN: 3.11.63, London, England
HEIGHT: 5 ft 9 (1 m 75)
CLUB SIDE: Arsenal (England)
EXPERIENCE: ★ ★ ★
KEY FACT: 100 per cent commitment.
AMAZING FACT: Has scored more goals for Arsenal than anyone else.

7 SUPER STRIKERS

DENMARK

NAME: Per Pederson
BORN: 30.3.69, Ålborg, Denmark
HEIGHT: 6 ft 1 (1 m 86)
CLUB SIDE: Blackburn Rovers (England)
EXPERIENCE: ★
KEY FACT: Very fast, with a powerful left foot.
AMAZING FACT: His career was nearly ended by a motorbike accident.

NAME: Brian Laudrup
BORN: 22.2.69, Vienna, Austria
HEIGHT: 6 ft 1 (1 m 86)
CLUB SIDE: Glasgow Rangers (Scotland)
EXPERIENCE: ★ ★ ★ ★ ★
KEY FACT: Can dribble at high speed.
AMAZING FACT: His brother Michael and father Finn have both been Denmark's Footballer of the Year.

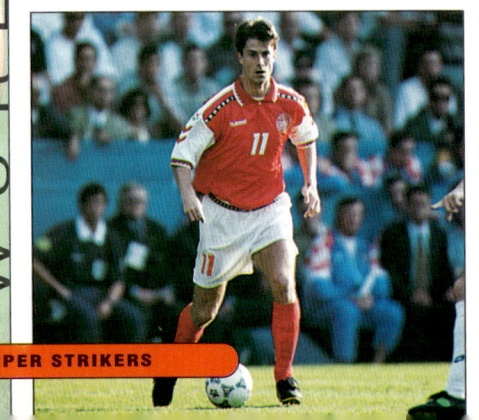

8 SUPER STRIKERS

ITALY

NAME: Alessandro Del Piero
BORN: 9.11.74, Conegliano, Italy
HEIGHT: 5 ft 8 (1 m 73)
CLUB SIDE: Juventus (Italy)
EXPERIENCE: ★ ★
KEY FACT: Prolific goal scorer.
AMAZING FACT: Played nearly 100 games during the 1996–97 season for Juventus, his national side, the Under 21s and the army!

NAME: Gianfranco Zola
BORN: 5.7.66, Oliena, Sardinia
HEIGHT: 5 ft 5 (1 m 65)
CLUB SIDE: Chelsea (England)
EXPERIENCE: ★ ★ ★
KEY FACT: Free kick specialist.
AMAZING FACT: Took over Maradona's number 10 shirt at Napoli.

9 SUPER STRIKERS

NORWAY

NAME: Tore André Flo
BORN: 15.6.73, Sogndal, Norway
HEIGHT: 6 ft 2 (1 m 88)
CLUB SIDE: Chelsea (England)
EXPERIENCE: ★
KEY FACT: Good in the air and can shoot with both feet.
AMAZING FACT: Called 'Flo-Naldo' by Norwegian fans.

NAME: Egil Østenstad
BORN: 2.1.72, Haugesund, Norway
HEIGHT: 5 ft 11 (1 m 80)
CLUB SIDE: Southampton (England)
EXPERIENCE: ★
KEY FACT: Strong and quick.

10 SUPER STRIKERS

AUSTRIA

NAME: Dietmar Kuhbauer
BORN: 4.4.71, Heiligeutrcuz, Austria
HEIGHT: 5 ft 8 (1 m 73)
CLUB SIDE: Real Sociedad (Spain)
EXPERIENCE: ★ ★
KEY FACT: Very determined player with a powerful shot.

NAME: Anton 'Toni' Polster
BORN: 10.3.64, Vienna, Austria
HEIGHT: 6 ft 2 (1 m 88)
CLUB SIDE: Koln (Germany)
EXPERIENCE: ★ ★ ★ ★ ★
KEY FACT: Potent goal scorer with a powerful left foot.
AMAZING FACT: Austria's highest goal scorer of all time.

WORLD CUP 1998

11 SUPER STRIKERS

BULGARIA

NAME: Hristo Stoichkov
BORN: 8.2.66, Sofia, Bulgaria
HEIGHT: 5 ft 10 (1 m 78)
CLUB SIDE: Barcelona (Spain)
EXPERIENCE: ★ ★ ★ ★ ★
KEY FACT: Skilful and prolific goal scorer.
AMAZING FACT: Was the joint top scorer at USA '94.

NAME: Emil Kostadinov
BORN: 12.8.67, Sofia, Bulgaria
HEIGHT: 5 ft 11 (1 m 80)
CLUB SIDE: Bayern Munich (Germany)
EXPERIENCE: ★ ★ ★ ★ ★
KEY FACT: Goal poacher extraordinaire.
AMAZING FACT: Nephew of the former Bulgarian coach Dimitar Penev.

12 SUPER STRIKERS

SPAIN

NAME: Raul Gonzalez
BORN: 27.6.77, Madrid, Spain
HEIGHT: 5 ft 11 (1 m 80)
CLUB SIDE: Real Madrid (Spain)
EXPERIENCE: ★
KEY FACT: A natural when it comes to scoring goals.
AMAZING FACT: As a boy, he used to support Real Madrid's local rivals Athletico.

NAME: Narváez Machón – 'Kiko'
BORN: 26.4.72, Cadiz, Spain
HEIGHT: 6 ft 2 (1 m 89)
CLUB SIDE: Athletico Madrid (Spain)
EXPERIENCE: ★ ★
KEY FACT: Flashes of brilliance but can drift out of the game.
AMAZING FACT: Scored twice in the final of the 1992 Olympic Games.

13 SUPER STRIKERS

BELGIUM

NAME: Nico Van Kerckhoven
BORN: 14.12.70, Lier, Belgium
HEIGHT: 6 ft 2 (1 m 88)
CLUB SIDE: Lierse (Belgium)
EXPERIENCE: ★
KEY FACT: Awesome in the air.

NAME: Luis Oliveira
BORN: 24.4.69, São Luis, Brazil
HEIGHT: 5 ft 9 (1 m 75)
CLUB SIDE: Fiorentina (Italy)
EXPERIENCE: ★ ★
KEY FACT: Very fast and an expert dribbler.

HOLLAND

NAME: Dennis Bergkamp
BORN: 18.5.69, Amsterdam, Holland
HEIGHT: 6 ft (1 m 83)
CLUB SIDE: Arsenal (England)
EXPERIENCE: ★ ★ ★ ★ ★
KEY FACT: Great finisher.
AMAZING FACT: He is named after the former Scotland star Denis Law!

14 SUPER STRIKERS

HOLLAND

NAME: Patrick Kluivert
BORN: 1.7.76, Amsterdam, Holland
HEIGHT: 6 ft 2 (1 m 88)
CLUB SIDE: AC Milan (Italy)
EXPERIENCE: ★ ★
KEY FACT: On his day, world class.
AMAZING FACT: First joined Ajax when he was just eight years old.

WORLD CUP 1998

15 SUPER STRIKERS

YUGOSLAVIA

NAME: Predag Mijatovic
BORN: 16.1.69, Podgorica, Yugoslavia
HEIGHT: 5 ft 10 (1 m 78)
CLUB SIDE: Real Madrid (Spain)
EXPERIENCE: ★ ★ ★
KEY FACT: A creator as well as a taker.

NAME: Anton Drobnjak
BORN: 21.9.68, Bijelo Polje, Yugoslavia
HEIGHT: 6 ft 1 (1 m 85)
CLUB SIDE: Lens (France)
EXPERIENCE: ★
KEY FACT: Prolific marksman who is good in the air and has a great right foot.

ROMANIA

NAME: Ion Vladoiu
BORN: 5.11.68, Calinesti, Romania
HEIGHT: 5 ft 7 (1 m 70)
CLUB SIDE: FC Koln (Germany)
EXPERIENCE: ★ ★ ★
KEY FACT: Unselfish team player.

16 SUPER STRIKERS

ROMANIA

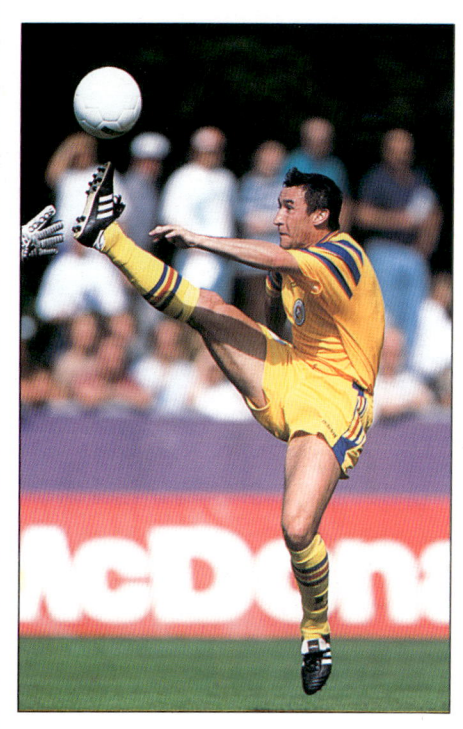

WORLD CUP 1998

NAME: Viorel Dinu Moldovan
BORN: 8.7.72, Bistrita, Romania
HEIGHT: 5 ft 9 (1 m 75)
CLUB SIDE: Coventry City (England)
EXPERIENCE: ★ ★
KEY FACT: Very hard-working with a good turn of pace.

17 SUPER STRIKERS

GERMANY

NAME: Jürgen Klinsmann
BORN: 30.7.64, Göppingen, Germany
HEIGHT: 6 ft 1 (1 m 85)
CLUB SIDE: Tottenham Hotspur (England)
EXPERIENCE: ★ ★ ★ ★ ★
KEY FACT: Has a good eye for goal.
AMAZING FACT: He was voted German Footballer of the Year in 1994, and then English Footballer of the Year in 1995!

NAME: Fredi Bobic
BORN: 30.10.71, Maribor, Slovenia
HEIGHT: 6 ft 2 (1 m 88)
CLUB SIDE: Stuttgart (Germany)
EXPERIENCE: ★ ★
KEY FACT: A fearless forward.

18 SUPER STRIKERS

CROATIA

NAME: Davor Suker
BORN: 1.1.68, Osijek, Croatia
HEIGHT: 6 ft 2 (1 m 88)
CLUB SIDE: Real Madrid (Spain)
EXPERIENCE: ★ ★ ★
KEY FACT: Phenomenal goal scorer.

NAME: Alen Boksic
BORN: 31.1.70, Makarska, Croatia
HEIGHT: 6 ft 2 (1 m 88)
CLUB SIDE: Lazio (Italy)
EXPERIENCE: ★ ★ ★
KEY FACT: Makes as many goals as he scores.
AMAZING FACT: Won a European Cup Winners' medal with Marseille in 1983 and was top goal scorer in the French league in the same season.

19 SUPER STRIKERS

SCOTLAND

NAME: Duncan Ferguson
BORN: 22.12.71, Stirling, Scotland
HEIGHT: 6 ft 4 (1 m 93)
CLUB SIDE: Everton (England)
EXPERIENCE: ★
KEY FACT: Superb in the air.

NAME: Gordon Durie
BORN: 6.12.65, Paisley, Scotland
HEIGHT: 6 ft (1 m 83)
CLUB SIDE: Glasgow Rangers (Scotland)
EXPERIENCE: ★ ★ ★
KEY FACT: Goal poacher.
AMAZING FACT: Once scored five goals in a match for Chelsea against Walsall.

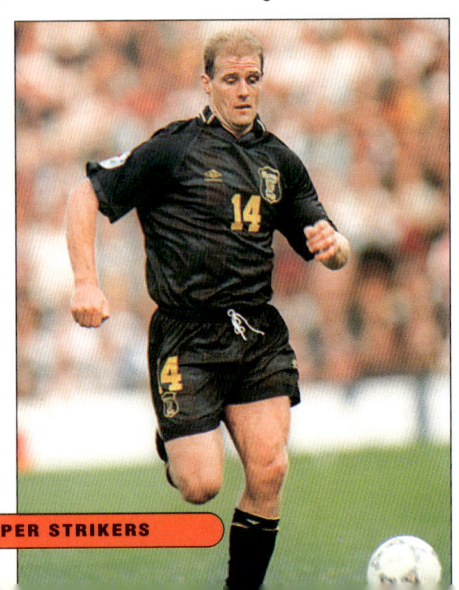

20 SUPER STRIKERS

NIGERIA

NAME: Daniel Amokachi
BORN: 30.12.72, Kaduna, Nigeria
HEIGHT: 5 ft 10 (1 m 78)
CLUB SIDE: Besiktas (Turkey)
EXPERIENCE: ★ ★ ★
KEY FACT: A strong and powerful natural goal scorer.
AMAZING FACT: The youngest ever player to appear in the African Nations Cup.

NAME: Emmanual Amunike
BORN: 25.12.70, Ezebodo, Nigeria
HEIGHT: 5 ft 9 (1 m 75)
CLUB SIDE: Barcelona (Spain)
EXPERIENCE: ★ ★
KEY FACT: Loves to run at defenders.
AMAZING FACT: Scored the winning goal in the Olympic final against Argentina in Atlanta 1996.

21 SUPER STRIKERS

SOUTH AFRICA

NAME: Phil Masinga
BORN: 28.6.69, Johannesburg, South Africa
HEIGHT: 6 ft 2 (1 m 88)
CLUB SIDE: Bari (Italy)
EXPERIENCE: ★ ★ ★
KEY FACT: South Africa's top striker – on his day.
AMAZING FACT: Briefly retired from the national team after fans hurled abuse at him for bad performances.

22 SUPER STRIKERS

MOROCCO

NAME: Mohammed Fertoute
BORN: 7.7.70, Casablanca, Morocco
HEIGHT: 6 ft (1 m 83)
CLUB SIDE: Wydad Casablanca (Morocco)
EXPERIENCE: ★ ★

TUNISIA

NAME: Adel Sellimi
BORN: 16.11.72, Mahdia, Tunisia
HEIGHT: 5 ft 11 (1 m 80)
CLUB SIDE: Nantes (France)
EXPERIENCE: ★ ★ ★ ★
KEY FACT: His goals will be the key to Tunisia's success.

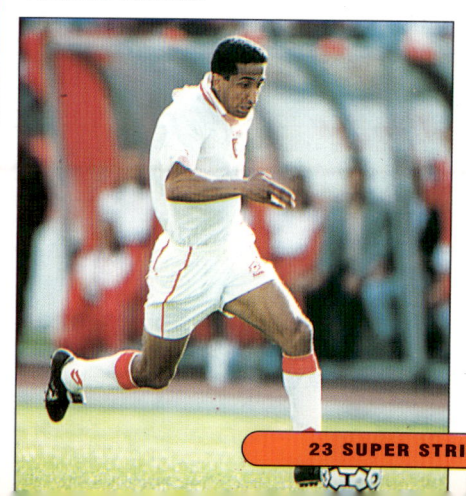

23 SUPER STRIKERS

CAMEROON

NAME: Alphonse Tchami
BORN: 14.2.71, Yaoundé, Cameroon
HEIGHT: 5 ft 11 (1 m 80)
CLUB SIDE: Hertha Berlin (Germany)
EXPERIENCE: ★ ★ ★ ★
KEY FACT: Watch out for his speed and a great shot.
AMAZING FACT: Used to play with Maradona at Boca Juniors in Argentina.

NAME: Patrick Mboma
BORN: 1.7.76, Nkenglicock, Cameroon
HEIGHT: 6 ft 1 (1 m 85)
CLUB SIDE: Gambo Osaka (Japan)
EXPERIENCE: ★

COLOMBIA

NAME: Antony de Avila
BORN: 21.12.61, Santa María, Colombia
HEIGHT: 5 ft 3 (1 m 61)
CLUB SIDE: New Jersey Metrostars (USA)
EXPERIENCE: ★ ★ ★ ★ ★
KEY FACT: Makes as many goals as he scores.
AMAZING FACT: Nicknamed 'Smurf' because of his height.

24 SUPER STRIKERS

COLOMBIA

NAME: Faustino Asprilla
BORN: 10.11.69, Tuluá, Colombia
HEIGHT: 5 ft 9 (1 m 75)
CLUB SIDE: Parma (Italy)
EXPERIENCE: ★ ★
KEY FACT: His goals are vital to the team's success.
AMAZING FACT:
Was once banned by the Colombian FA for leaving his hotel without permission. The other players eventually managed to persuade the FA to let him play again because they didn't want to play without his fire power up front!

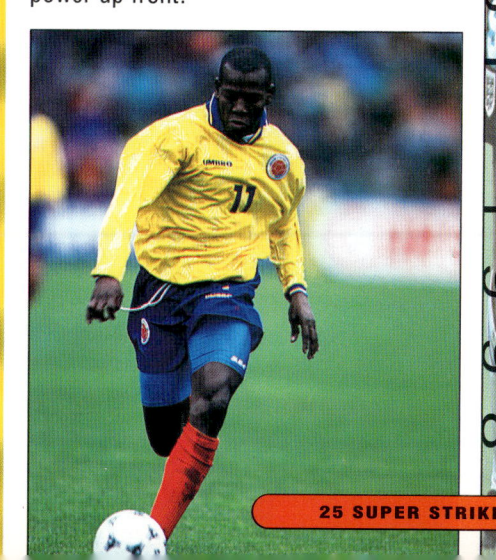

WORLD CUP 1998

25 SUPER STRIKERS

PARAGUAY

NAME: Jose Cardozo
BORN: 19.3.71, Nueva Italia, Paraguay
HEIGHT: 6 ft (1 m 83)
CLUB SIDE: Necaxa (Paraguay)
EXPERIENCE: ★ ★
KEY FACT: Very motivated after being left out of the side for over a year.

NAME: Derlis Soto
BORN: 4.3.73, Caaguazú, Paraguay
HEIGHT: 5 ft 8 (1 m 73)
CLUB SIDE: Guarani (Paraguay)
EXPERIENCE: ★
KEY FACT: Robust forward who likes to put his weight about.

CHILE

NAME: Ivan Zamorano
BORN: 18.1.67, Santiago, Chile
HEIGHT: 5 ft 10 (1 m 78)
CLUB SIDE: Inter Milan (Italy)
EXPERIENCE: ★ ★ ★ ★
KEY FACT: Mixes grace with speed and bravery.

26 SUPER STRIKERS

CHILE

WORLD CUP 1998

NAME: Marcelo Salas
BORN: 24.12.74, Temuco, Chile
HEIGHT: 5 ft 9 (1 m 75)
CLUB SIDE: River Plate (Argentina)
EXPERIENCE: ★ ★ ★
KEY FACT: Robust and powerful goal machine.
AMAZING FACT: Nicknamed 'El Matador' – the Bullfighter.

27 SUPER STRIKERS

ARGENTINA

NAME: Hernan Crespo
BORN: 5.7.75, Buenos Aires, Argentina
HEIGHT: 6 ft 1 (1 m 85)
CLUB SIDE: Parma (Italy)
EXPERIENCE: ★ ★
KEY FACT: The fire power in the Argentine attack.

NAME: Gabriel Batistuta
BORN: 1.2.69, Reconquista, Argentina
HEIGHT: 6 ft 1 (1 m 85)
CLUB SIDE: Fiorentina (Italy)
EXPERIENCE: ★ ★ ★ ★
KEY FACT: Free kick expert.
AMAZING FACT: Argentina's top goal scorer of all time.

28 SUPER STRIKERS

MEXICO

NAME: Luis Hernandez
BORN: 22.12.68, Mexico City, Mexico
HEIGHT: 5 ft 9 (1 m 75)
CLUB SIDE: Necaxa (Mexico)
EXPERIENCE: ★ ★ ★
KEY FACT: Mexico's goal machine.
AMAZING FACT: Scored the 2000th ever goal in the Copa America Championship 1997.

JAMAICA

NAME: Deon Burton
BORN: 25.10.76, Ashford, England
HEIGHT: 5 ft 8 (1 m 73)
CLUB SIDE: Derby County (England)
EXPERIENCE: ★
KEY FACT: Big, strong and fast.
AMAZING FACT: On qualifying for the finals he said: "Fairy tale doesn't seem a big enough word for what has happened."

29 SUPER STRIKERS

USA

NAME:
Eric Wynalda
BORN:
6.9.69, California, USA
HEIGHT:
6 ft 1 (1 m 85)
CLUB SIDE:
San Jose Clash (USA)
EXPERIENCE:
★ ★ ★ ★ ★
KEY FACT:
Team penalty taker who is also strong in the air.

NAME: Joe Max Moore
BORN: 2.3.71, Tulsa, USA
HEIGHT: 5 ft 9 (1 m 75)
CLUB SIDE: New England Revolution (USA)
EXPERIENCE: ★ ★ ★ ★
KEY FACT: Scores vital goals from all around the penalty box.
AMAZING FACT: Scored four goals against El Salvador in 1993 – the first US player to score so many since 1934.

30 SUPER STRIKERS

IRAN

NAME: Ali Daei
BORN: 21.3.69, Ardabīl, Iran
HEIGHT: 6 ft 2 (1 m 88)
CLUB SIDE: Arminia Bielefeld (Germany)
EXPERIENCE: ★ ★ ★
KEY FACT: One of the most lethal strikers in the world.

JAPAN

NAME: Kazu Miura
BORN: 26.2.67, Shiga, Japan
HEIGHT: 5 ft 9 (1 m 75)
CLUB SIDE: Verdy Kawasaki (Japan)
EXPERIENCE: ★ ★ ★ ★ ★
KEY FACT: Japan's ace striker.
AMAZING FACT: Scored six goals in the 10-0 rout of Macao.

NAME: Lopes Wagner
BORN: 29.1.69, Rio de Janeiro, Brazil
HEIGHT: 6 ft (1 m 83)
CLUB SIDE: Bellmare Hiratsuka (Japan)
EXPERIENCE: ★
KEY FACT: Can shoot with either foot and adds some height to the Japanese attack.

31 SUPER STRIKERS

SAUDI ARABIA

NAME: Sami Al Jaber
BORN: 1972
HEIGHT: 5 ft 9 (1 m 75)
CLUB SIDE: Al Hilal (Saudi Arabia)
EXPERIENCE: ★ ★ ★ ★ ★
KEY FACT: Pacey and loves to run at defenders.
AMAZING FACT: Would probably be playing overseas by now, but the Saudi Arabian league doesn't allow its players to play abroad.

SOUTH KOREA

NAME: Choi Yong-Soo
BORN: 10.8.73, Pusan, South Korea
HEIGHT: 6 ft (1 m 83)
CLUB SIDE: Sangmoo (South Korea)
EXPERIENCE: ★ ★
KEY FACT: Very focused on his game and can shoot and head the ball with power.
AMAZING FACT: Scored the most goals (seven) in the final stages of the Asian World Cup qualifying competition.

32 SUPER STRIKERS